THE 100 MOST MOST

INTERESTING

CHINESE CHARACTERS

www.royalcollins.com

THE 100 MOST MOST INTERESTING CHINESE CHARACTERS

XU HUI

TRANSLATED BY JULIE LOO

Chemical Industry Press

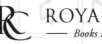
ROYAL COLLINS
Books Beyond Boundaries

The 100 Most Interesting Chinese Characters

Xu Hui
Translated by Julie Loo

First published in 2022 by Royal Collins Publishing Group Inc.
Groupe Publication Royal Collins Inc.
BKM Royalcollins Publishers Private Limited

Headquarters: 550-555 boul. René-Lévesque O Montréal (Québec) H2Z1B1 Canada
India office: 805 Hemkunt House, 8th Floor, Rajendra Place, New Delhi 110008

Original Edition © Chemical Industry Press

ISBN: 978-1-4878-0770-2

To find out more about our publications, please visit www.royalcollins.com.

As well as its obvious visual appeal, China's millennia-old writing system is a carrier of the nation's culture and identity. In this book, Xu Hui selects and explains the 100 most interesting Chinese characters with the help of eye-catching illustrations that bring their meanings alive, and historic tracings through seal script all the way back to ancient oracle bone carvings. For novices and experts alike, this translation by Julie Loo offers English readers a compelling insight into the world of written Chinese.

儿 child, son [ér]

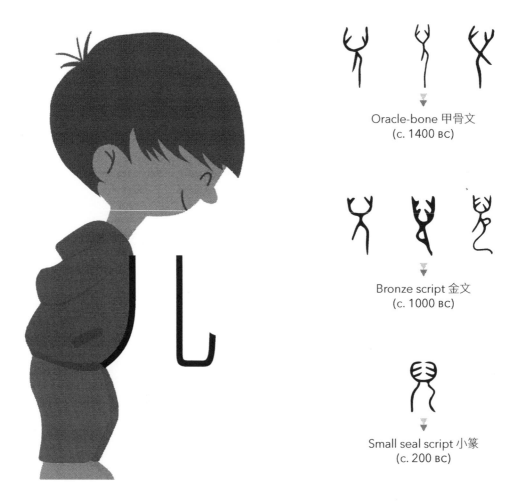

Oracle-bone 甲骨文
(c. 1400 BC)

Bronze script 金文
(c. 1000 BC)

Small seal script 小篆
(c. 200 BC)

- The complex form of the character for *child/son* is a pictographic character. The bottom part of the oracle bone script was character's symbol for a person. According to the *Book of Rites*, when a baby boy was three months old, he would get his first haircut, leaving a corner of hair on his head. This hairstyle was only for sons.
- *Shuowen Jiezi Dictionary*: 儿 refers to *child*, with the shape of the character resembling the infant's fontanel, which has not yet closed.
- In ancient times, boys were referred to as 儿 *son*, while girls were referred to as 婴 [yīng] *infant*.

门 door [mén]

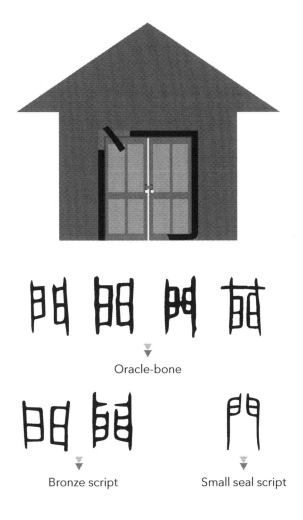

Oracle-bone

Bronze script   Small seal script

- The complex character for door is a photographic character resembling two doors. Each half is a 户 [hù] *household*.
- In ancient times, 衡门 [héng mén] referred to *the simple dwelling of a recluse*.
- In the *Five Rites of Ancient China*, one of the ritual ceremonies was the Worship of the Door Spirit. Ban Gu, a famous historian and literary scholar in the Eastern Han Dynasty, remarked in the classic *Baihu Tongyi*, "Autumn is the time to worship the Door. The door protects when shut. Autumn is also the season when the harvest is ripe. Self-providence and self-protection." The dog's sacrificial role in the Worship of the Door Spirit is to guard the door.

卫 guard [wèi]

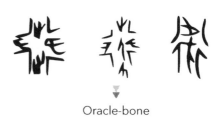

Oracle-bone

Bronze script

Small seal script

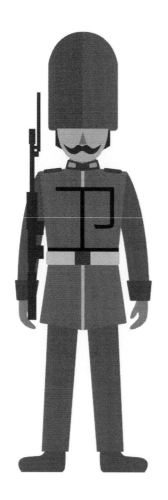

- This is compound ideographic character. The character image of the oracle bone script was four right angles that represented a cross junction. The four 'legs' in the center represented the people guarding the road.
- *Shuowen Jiezi Dictionary*: 卫 is also 宿卫 [sù wèi] meaning *a guard that stays the night*, referring to *the imperial guard* or *palace guard*. In the past, the palace guards had to stay overnight on the night shift. 卫 also denotes *fletching - the feather on an arrow.*
- 卫 was also another name for *the donkey*, which was used by guards in ancient times.

夫 husband [fū]

Oracle-bone

Bronze script

Small seal script

- This is a pictographic character meaning *husband*. The character's symbol of the oracle bone script was a person standing erect with a horizontal stroke at the top to represent a hair pin.
- In ancient China, men became adults at the age of twenty during the capping ceremony, after which they were ready to take on the role of a husband. At the age of seventy, a man would receive the title 老夫 [lǎo fū] *an elder*.
- The title for *adult men* in the past was 夫. A man who is married is called 丈夫 [zhàng fū], *husband*. His *wife* is the 夫人 [fū rén] *person belonging to the husband*.
- The *ordinary man* is called a 匹夫 [pǐ fū].

屯 station [tún]

| Oracle-bone | Bronze script | Small seal script |

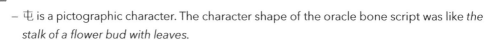

- 屯 is a pictographic character. The character shape of the oracle bone script was like *the stalk of a flower bud with leaves.*
- The original meaning of this character is *difficulty, hardship.*
- The *place where the military troop gathers and stations* is 屯. In ancient China, the 屯田 [tún tián] system was set up to cultivate wasteland into food-producing land to feed the military. This involved three groups of people – military troops, peasants without land, and traders.

◻ district, area [qū]

Oracle-bone

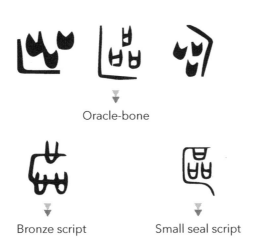

Bronze script   Small seal script

- The complex character ◻ written as 區 is a compound ideograph. The character's symbol of its oracle bone script was a vessel for keeping things in. Within the vessel were three squares to represent its obligations.
- As the idea of ◻ is that it is able to contain a lot. It is extended to refer to *district, distinguish.*

专　to monopolize, to take sole possession [zhuān]

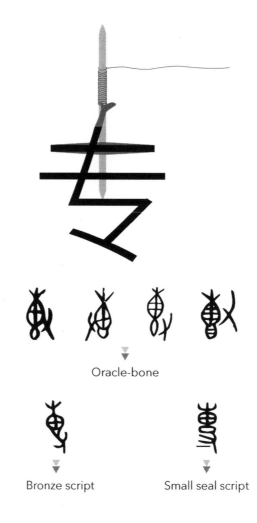

Oracle-bone

Bronze script　　　Small seal script

- The complex form of the character is a compound ideograph. The character's symbol on the right side of its oracle bone script was a hand, and on the left was the symbol for a weaving brick.
- In ancient times, the character 专 referred to the brick used for weaving.
- Used metaphorically in 专一 [zhuān yī] *single minded / undivided* and 专断 [zhuān duàn] *to act arbitrarily*.

比 to compare [bǐ]

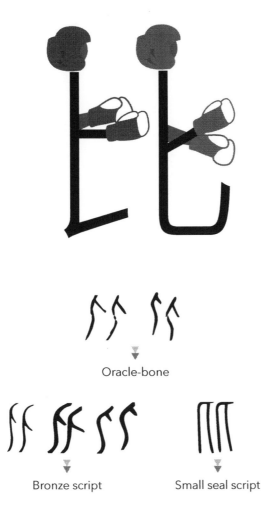

Oracle-bone

Bronze script   Small seal script

- The character for 比 is a pictographic character denoting two people standing or walking together. The idea indicated closeness.
- In the phrase 比较 [bǐ jiào] *contrast*, the left part of the character 较 is a 车 [jū] *carriage*. The horizontal bars are the objects of competition. The right part of the character consists of two people competing, bringing out the meaning of *contrast*.

贝 shell [bèi]

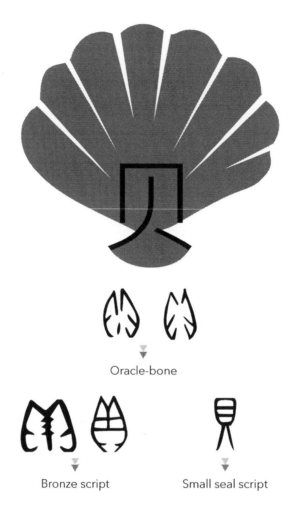

Oracle-bone

Bronze script   Small seal script

- This is a pictographic character. Its oracle bone script was the character that symbolized a shell.
- 贝 referred to a sea shell, namely the cowrie shell.
- People in ancient times traded with shells. During the Zhou Dynasty, metal coins replaced shells as the medium of payment. From the Qin Period, the term 钱 [qián] *money* began to denote the items used in payment.

夭 tender, young [yāo]

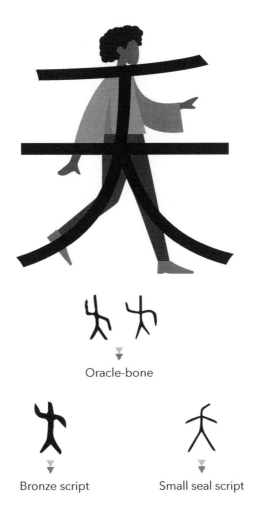

Oracle-bone

Bronze script

Small seal script

- This is a pictographic character. It looks like a person swinging their arms as they walk.
- It is extended to mean *submit/subdue*. It is also used to mean *premature death*.
- It also refers to *a new born animal or plant*. Two of these characters are put together in the phrase 桃之夭夭 [táo zhī yāo yāo] to mean *a young thriving peach plant about to bloom lushly*.

介 armour, to be situated in between [jiè]

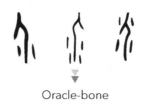

Oracle-bone

Large seal script
籀文 (c. 700 BC)

Small seal script

– This is a pictographic character. Its oracle bone script was the character that symbolized a person in armour.
– Zhou Yafu led the army in the city of Xiliu. When the Emperor Wen of the Han Dynasty went to visit the troops, Zhou Yafu made a bow with his hands clasped and said, "介冑之士 [jiè zhòu zhī shì] *Warriors in armor* do not worship; please allow the military salute." The Emperor was impressed with his strict adherence to military rules.
– The extended meaning is *to intervene*. Another meaning is *to introduce*.

仆 servant [pú]

Oracle-bone

Bronze script

Small seal script

- The complex character for *servant* is a compound ideograph, referring to a person serving another.
- In ancient times, people were divided into ten ranks, the lowest of which were *servant* ranking in ninth position and *slave* ranking tenth.
- When addressing oneself in front of the emperor in imperial times, the first-person pronoun was to be avoided as a show of humility. Dukes and princes used the pronoun 臣 [chén] *subject*, while ministers, nobles, and officials used the pronoun 仆 *servant*.

storehouse, granary [cāng]

Oracle-bone   Bronze script   Small seal script

– The complex character is a pictographic character. Its character's symbol in the oracle bone script was a cover with a vertical line underneath, resembling a wall separating smaller sections. The figure at the bottom looked like a little wooden exit door.

– "Grains are stored in a 仓 *storehouse/granary* and rice is stored in a 廪 [lǐn] *granary*."

– Two common folk adages in China, 抢收 [qiǎng shōu] *rush in the harvest* and 抢秋 [qiǎng qiū] *rush in the fall*, have extended the meaning of the character when combined with other single characters to mean *in a tearing hurry*.

– In ancient times, a round shaped storehouse for grains was called 囷 [qūn] *a barn*. A square shaped storehouse was called 仓 *a granary*. Storage for military weapons was called 库 [kù] *an arsenal*, and the place where books were stored was called 府 [fǔ] *a library*.

火 fire [huǒ]

Oracle-bone

Bronze script

Small seal script

- This is a pictographic character. "*Fire* varies in forms. Even in its varied forms, it can destroy, damage, or change the forms of others." The oracle bone script was a symbol of three fiery flames flaring up from the ground.
- The hand-drill fire-making technique used in primitive times required wood to be changed according to the seasons, giving the actions new names. 改火 [gǎi huǒ] *change of fire* and 改木 [gǎi mù] *change of wood* both meant *time to change*.
- In the Northern Wei Military System, each group of ten soldiers was called a 火 'fire' and they had to share one stove. To cook their meals, they needed to build fire. That was how the term 火伴 [huǒ bàn] *'fire companions'* [buddies] was derived.

正 straight, positive [zhèng]

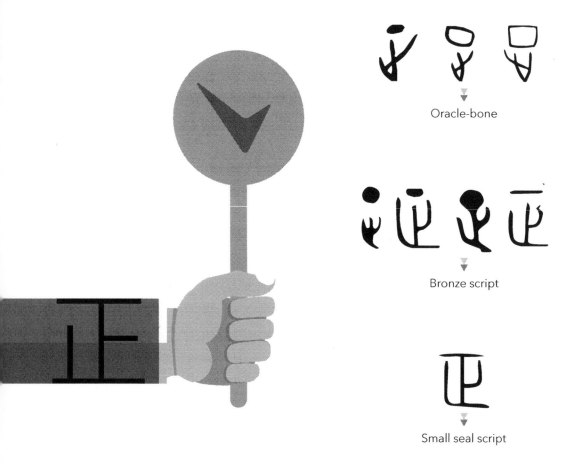

Oracle-bone

Bronze script

Small seal script

– This is a compound ideographic character. It denotes *right and proper, to correct a wrong,* and *to possess a pure and righteous spirit.*
– It is used for the first month of the year, 正月 [zhēng yuè] – the first month of the Spring Festival. *The first year of the reign of an emperor* was called 元年 [yuán nián] and the *first month* of his accession was 正月.

旦 day, dawn [dàn]

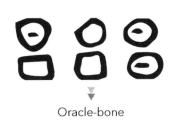

Oracle-bone

Bronze script

Small seal script

- This is a compound ideographic character. The character's symbol for its oracle bone script was a sun. Below it was its shadow, to denote *dawn, night has passed and the sun is rising, daybreak*.
- "The wife said that the rooster has crowed; dawn has come." The character 旦 used in this line describes the situation pictographically.
- The character is extended to mean the first day of every month in the lunar calendar.
- It is also used in traditional Chinese opera to address female artistes.

field, farm [tián]

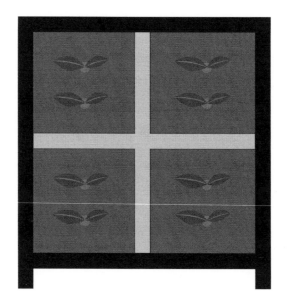

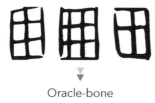

Oracle-bone

Bronze script

Small seal script

- This is a pictographic character. The outer frame in its oracle bone script depicted its purpose, namely to keep animals in. The horizontal and vertical lines inside the frame indicated the different segmented areas for hunting.
- The original purpose of 田 *field* was for hunting. The character was extended to mean farmland for the cultivation of vegetables.

史 an official in charge of historical records and events in ancient times [shǐ]

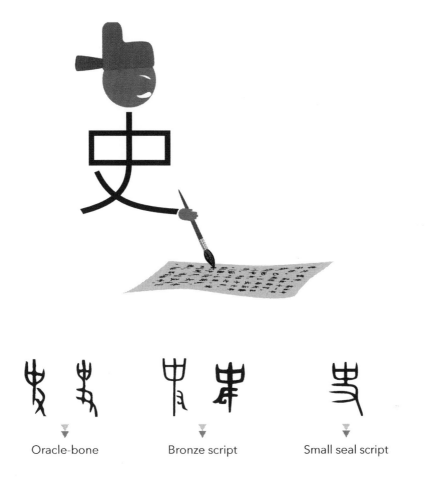

| Oracle-bone | Bronze script | Small seal script |

- 史 is a compound ideograph denoting a hand holding a hunting weapon. The character's symbol in its oracle bone script was the image of a hand holding a simplified form of a hunting weapon.
- The original idea of the character referred to the person who managed a hunting activity, or the person who kept a record of a hunt. Its meaning was later extended to the official who kept records of the country's events.
- To record words and actions were the two main jobs of this official.

央 central, to entreat [yāng]

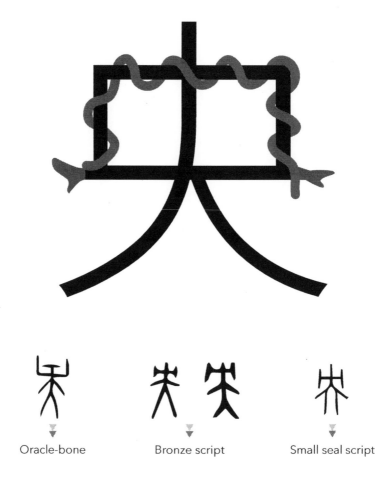

Oracle-bone   Bronze script   Small seal script

- This is a pictographic character. The character's symbol in the oracle bone script was a person standing erect. On his neck was a cangue, denoting a form of punishment. Extending from the original meaning, it was used to mean *middle and central*.
- The character by itself can mean *the middle half* or *the middle to the end*.
- From the original meaning of a punishment, the character thereupon combines with other characters to mean *to plead, to entreat*.

 used, former [jiù]

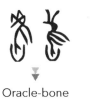

Oracle-bone

Bronze script

Small seal script

- This is a compound ideographic character that resembles an owl. The character's symbol in the oracle bone script was a bird with ear tufts and two large eyes. Below it was its nest. The idea of the character was extended to mean *a long time*.
- When the character is used to refer to the past, or to the original state, it usually encompasses some degree of positivity.

矢 arrow [shǐ]

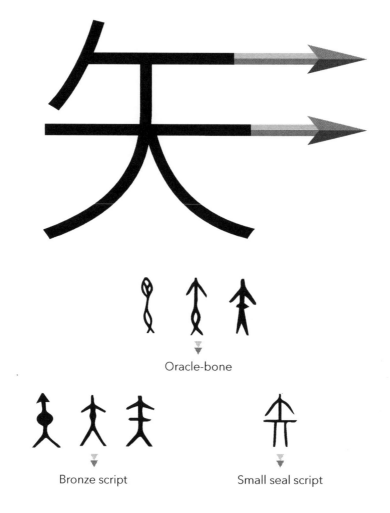

Oracle-bone

Bronze script   Small seal script

- This is a pictographic character. The oracle bone script contained the character's symbol of an arrowhead at the top. In the middle was the shaft, and at the end was the tail. In ancient times, it was said that "The arrow, drawn from the crossbow, has an arrowhead and feather at the end of it."
- According to records in *The Rites of Zhou*, an ancient Chinese work, there was an office for the manager of infantry archery. This person had to master the various methods of archery and the use of the different types of bows and arrows.
- 矢 has the same sound as 誓 [shì] *vow*. The line, "Living alone, yet never forgetting my vow" is commonly used.

印 to stamp, to print [yìn]

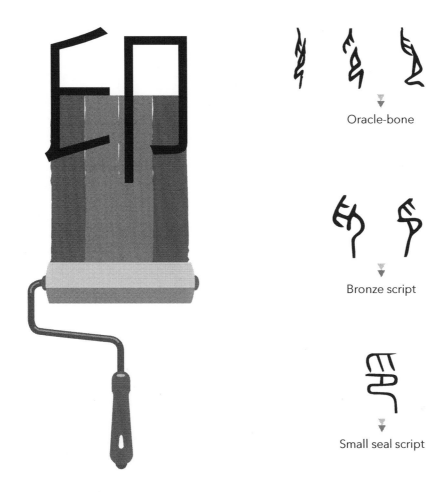

Oracle-bone

Bronze script

Small seal script

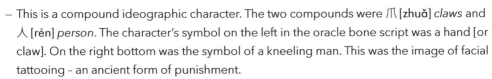

- This is a compound ideographic character. The two compounds were 爪 [zhuǎ] *claws* and 人 [rén] *person*. The character's symbol on the left in the oracle bone script was a hand [or claw]. On the right bottom was the symbol of a kneeling man. This was the image of facial tattooing - an ancient form of punishment.
- The term 印堂 [yìn táng] *ophryon* emerged from this form of punishment.
- The extended meaning of 印章 [yìn zhāng] *stamp* came from the criminal's facial tattoo.

召 to summon, to call [zhào]

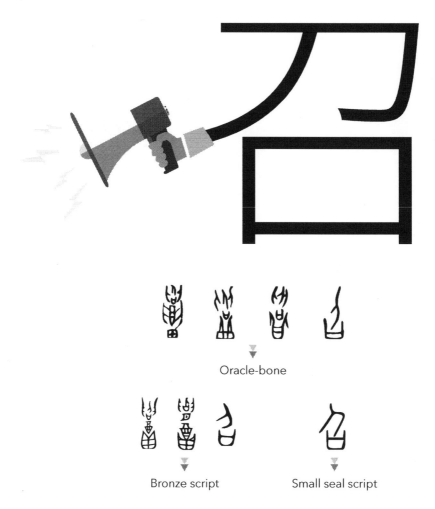

Oracle-bone

Bronze script   Small seal script

- The oracle bone version of this character reflected ancient etiquette for the hosting of banquets and any form of feast.
- This is a compound ideographic character, to mean inviting guests to a feast.
- The original meaning of the character was to *summon or invite* divine beings. It was later used for people. Its extended meaning is 召见 [zhào jiàn] *to summon or call in a subordinate*, 召唤 [zhào huàn] *to beckon*, or 召呼 [zhào hū] *to inform*.

出 to go out [chū]

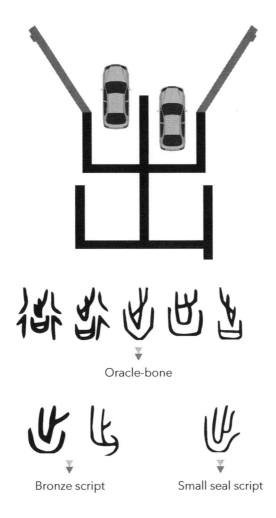

Oracle-bone

Bronze script   Small seal script

- 出 is a compound ideographic character. The oracle bone script was the figure of a cross junction. In the middle was a foot, and below it was the symbol for a dwelling place. It denotes a person leaving their place of residence.
- In ancient times, if a wife disobeyed her parents or committed any of the *seven sins*, her husband could *divorce* her 出妻 [chū qī]. This reflected one aspect of the ancient marriage system.
- 出阁 [chū gé] is often mistakenly written as 出閤 [chū gé] *to marry*. The three gateways in the imperial palace were 闱 [wéi] *a side gate*, 闺 [guī] *a small gate or a woman's bedroom*, and 閤 [gé] *a small gate or a woman's chamber*. For a woman, marriage involved leaving her chamber.

吉 auspicious [jí]

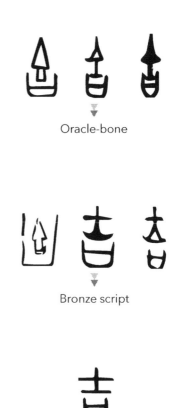

Oracle-bone

Bronze script

Small seal script

– This is a compound ideographic character, carrying the idea of *avoiding traps or pitfalls*. The opposite is falling into traps, which is 凶 [xiōng] *inauspicious*.

– 善 [shàn] *kind* is the extended meaning of 吉.

老 old [lǎo]

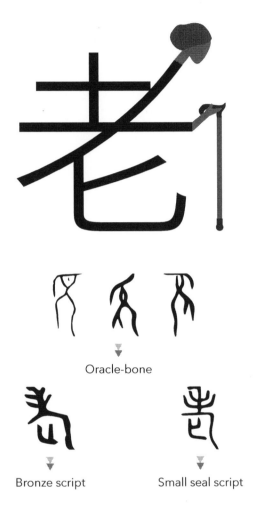

Oracle-bone

Bronze script   Small seal script

- This is a pictographic character. The oracle bone script was the image of a hunched person with long hair holding a walking stick.
- In ancient times, people were considered old when they reached the age of sixty. The three stages thereafter were 下寿 [xià shòu] *the age of sixty*, 中寿 [zhōng shòu] *the age of eighty*, and 上寿 [shàng shòu] *the age of a hundred*.
- During the Zhou Dynasty, the village, county, and prefecture established an appointment called 三老 [sān lǎo] - an official aged above fifty to be in charge of culture. His job was to educate. Subsequently, the office was developed into a system - the 三老五更 [sān lǎo wǔ gēng] system, appointing elderly and very experienced men in the county to the role.

死 to die, death [sǐ]

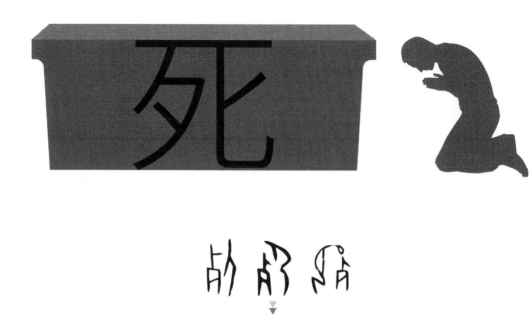

Oracle-bone

Bronze script   Small seal script

– This is a compound ideographic character. On the right side of the oracle bone script was a person with his body bowing over a corpse on the left. This was an image of mourning.
– The practice of second burial was common in ancient times. Many years after the first burial in the ground, the bones were unearthed and placed in either a coffin or earthenware for a second burial.

戎 army, military affairs [róng]

Oracle-bone

Bronze script

Small seal script

- This is a pictographic character. The character's symbol on the right of the oracle bone script was a dagger. On the left was a shield. The character referred to the standard equipment of a soldier in ancient times.
- 戎 was later used as the general term for military equipment and chariots.
- The kingdoms in the Central Plains used the term 戎 to refer to the minority tribes in the western regions. It was a neutral statement at first. However, a negative connotation became attached to the character during the Eastern Han Dynasty.

尧 tall [yáo]

Oracle-bone   Ancient text 古文   Small seal script

- The complex form of this character is a pictographic, resembling a person balancing two pottery vessels on his head.
- Emperor Yao took this character as his reign name. In doing so, he emphasized the significance of its image to his people, namely to take pride in the production of pottery.

光 light [guāng]

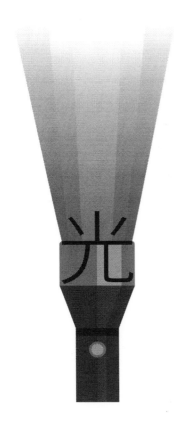

Oracle-bone

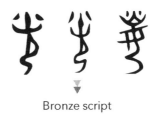

Bronze script

Small seal script

- This is a compound ideographic character. The oracle bone image was a person kneeling. Above his head was the symbol for flames. The idea was using fire to produce brightness. It reflected the use of candles for light in ancient times.
- "Fire burns when on the ground, but can be used as a torch when held."
- To use fire as light, it must be raised. The image of a flame in the character 光 is raised high for brightness; it does not mean that the fire is on the man's head.

吊　sympathy, to condole [diào]

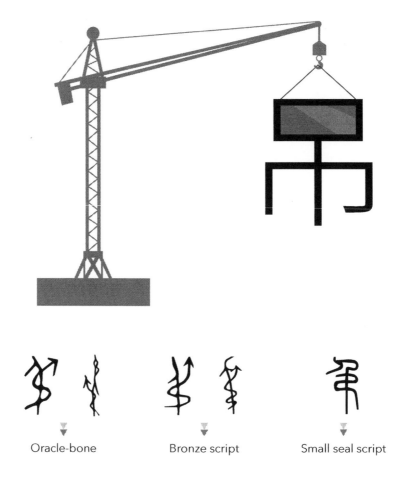

Oracle-bone　　　Bronze script　　　Small seal script

- 吊 is the popular form of the character 弔. It is a compound ideographic character denoting a son guarding the body of his deceased parent with a dart.
- In ancient times, the son of the deceased had to guard the body from animals. The dart in his hand was for the purpose of chasing animals away. The character was later extended to mean *to condole*.
- To show sympathy to the family of the deceased, the character 唁 [yàn] *condolence* is used. To show respect to the dead, 吊 is used.

自 self, oneself [zì]

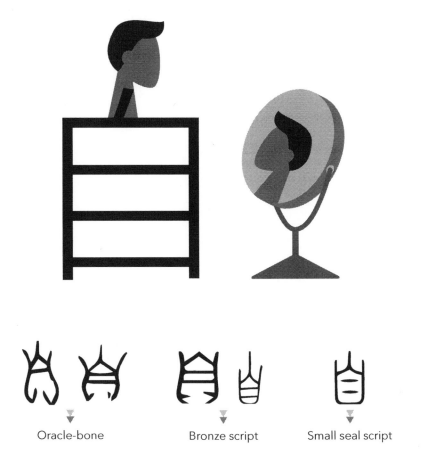

Oracle-bone

Bronze script

Small seal script

– This is a pictographic character. Its oracle bone script was the front view of a nose. The idea of the character was therefore *the nose*.
– The phrase 自尽 [zì jìn] originally meant that *one has completely expressed one's views*. Its meaning was later extended to indicate *taking one's own life*.

向 towards, direction [xiàng]

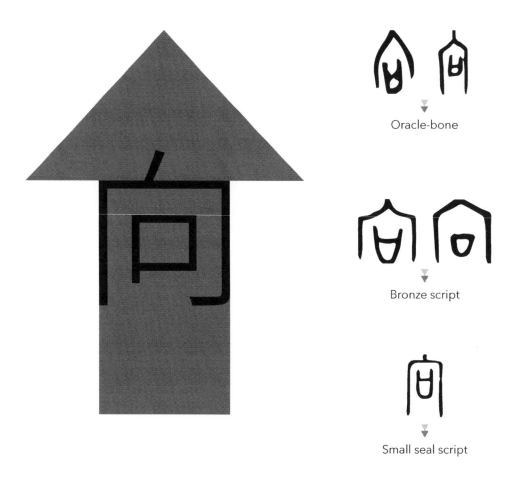

Oracle-bone

Bronze script

Small seal script

– This is a pictographic character. It originally referred to the open window on the north wall of a house. The character's symbol in oracle bone script was the roof of a house and the two walls. Below was the symbol representing a window. The ideographic meaning referred to the open window.

– In ancient terminology, 外向 [wài xiàng] *extroverted* and 内向 [nèi xiàng] *introverted* were totally different from modern-day definitions of the two words. 内向 was used for a man because his heart pointed towards home. The woman was 外向 because she had to leave her birth family and follow her husband when she married.

名 name [míng]

Oracle-bone

Bronze script

Small seal script

- This is a compound ideographic character, with the original idea of regarding oneself.
- When a child was three months old, his parents had to give him a name. It was considered rude for his peers, or older people who were not close to him, or the younger generation to address him by his personal name. To show him respect, they had to use his title. To address a person by his full name was a sign of disrespect.
- The proverbs 不名一钱 [bù míng yī qián] and 不名一文 [bù míng yì wén] meaning *penniless*, originated from the Han Dynasty official Deng Tong.
- The phrase 目上 [mù shàng] refers to *the point between the brow and the eyelashes*. The phrase 名目 [míng mù] *name of things* is still used in the present day.

字 character (word), title [zì]

Bronze script   Small seal script

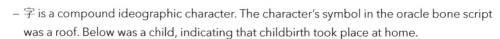

- 字 is a compound ideographic character. The character's symbol in the oracle bone script was a roof. Below was a child, indicating that childbirth took place at home.
- In ancient times, 文 [wén] *writing* was made up of lines crossing one another. The development of phono-semantic compound characters started when pictographic characters began to run out. This was the development of 字.
- People in ancient times used 字 *a title* to indicate their achievement. "A name refers to the self; a title reflects an achievement."
- Girls went through the coming-of-age ceremony at the age of fifteen in ancient times. The period after the ceremony was called 待字 [dài zì] *waiting for a title to be bestowed upon them*, meaning *waiting to be betrothed*.

行 to walk, to perform, to carry out [xíng]

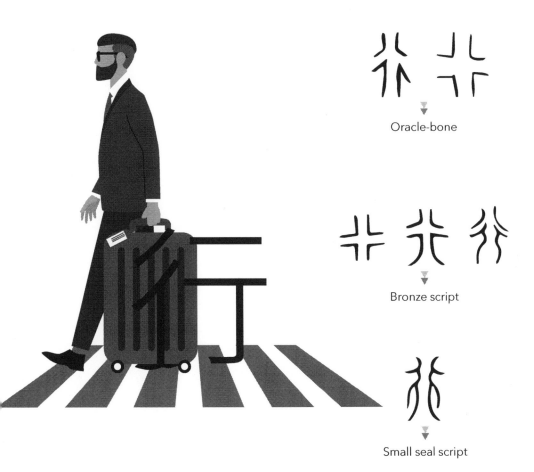

Oracle-bone

Bronze script

Small seal script

– This is a pictographic character carrying the idea of a cross junction. The image in the oracle bone script was a northern-south street with an east and a west exit.
– During the Spring and Autumn Period, every state had its own 行人 [xíng rén] *diplomats*. They were known as 行李 [xíng li] *envoys* when they went on diplomatic missions.

孙 grandson [sūn]

Oracle-bone

Bronze script

Small seal script

- This is a compound ideological character. The compounds in the character were 子 [zǐ] *son* and 系 [xì] *continuation of the lineage*. The oracle bone script was a son and a thin silk rope.
- In ancient times, the grandson was responsible for keeping vigil during the wake of his paternal grandfather. This tradition showed that the relationship between a grandfather and grandson was closer than between a father and son.
- 孙 was extended to mean *capillaries*.
- The character became a family name from the time of Wu Zhongyi, the grandson of Hui Sun, whose father was Wei Wugong.

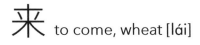 来 to come, wheat [lái]

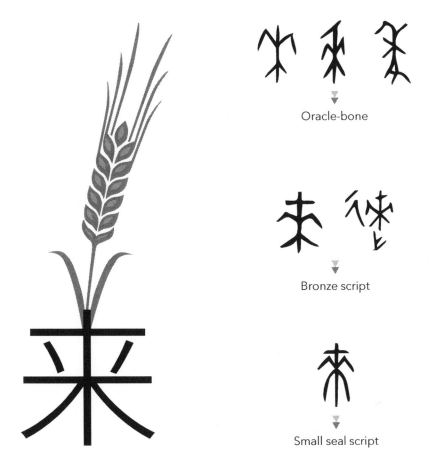

Oracle-bone

Bronze script

Small seal script

- The complex form of this character was a pictograph denoting a stalk of wheat. The original meaning of 来 was *wheat*.
- Wheat was originally produced in Western Asia. Four to five thousand years ago, it was brought into the western regions of China. The people of the Zhou Dynasty called it 贻我来牟 [yí wǒ lái móu] creating the image of *wheat as a foreign object*.

进 to advance, to move forward [jìn]

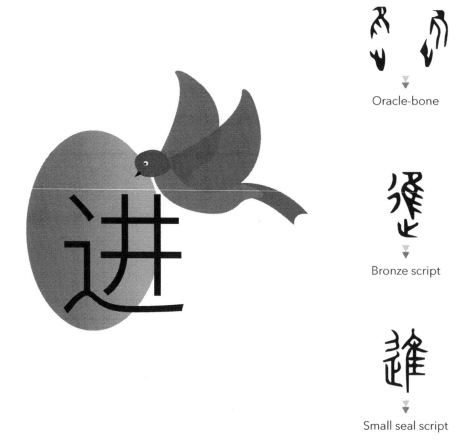

Oracle-bone

Bronze script

Small seal script

- The complex form of this character was pictograph denoting *ascension*. The character's symbol in the oracle bone script was a person's foot. Above it was a bird.
- 进 meant using a bird as a sacrificial offering with 璧 [bì] *a circular jade disk with a hole in the center*. Eventually, the meaning of 进 was extended to include *offer (in respect)*, and it evolved even further to refer to *moving forward*.
- An ancient saying stated, "In the situation of serving the emperor, it is very difficult to be promoted, but to leave the job is easy. There is protocol for the different positions. However, if it were easy to get a promotion and hard to leave a post, then chaos would ensue. To avoid such chaos, promotion should be made hard and leaving made easy."
- The title of 进士 [jìn shì] *a successful candidate in the highest imperial examinations* was in existence as early as the Zhou Dynasty, or even before.

县 to hang [xiàn]

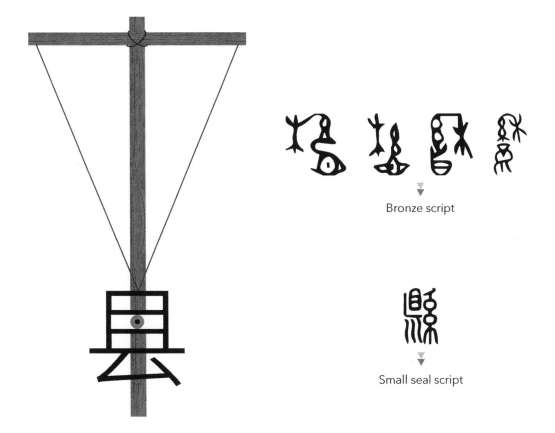

Bronze script

Small seal script

- The complex form of this character is a compound ideograph. The character's symbol on the left of the oracle bone script was wood. The top right was a rope and the bottom was a head, indicating that the head of a person was hung on the wooden pole as a public warning.
- The use of *displaying the head of an executed criminal as a warning to the public* was the exact picture of this character.

吹 to blow [chuī]

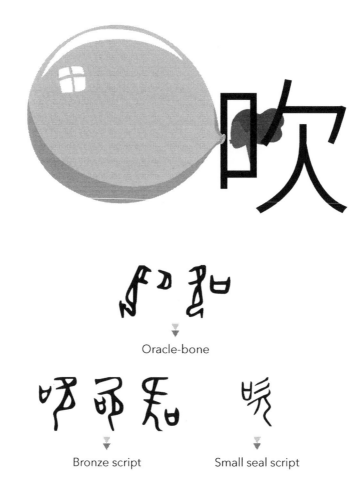

Oracle-bone

Bronze script

Small seal script

- This is a compound ideographic character. When a person blows out air, he first has to open his mouth to take it in. The idea of the character was a mouth opened to blow air out.
- There is a difference between 吹 to blow and 嘘 [xū] to breathe air out slowly. 吹 requires fast action. It is combined with other characters to mean boast or be in a draught as well as other phrases. 嘘 is a slow movement resulting in the air blown out being warm. Consequently, it is used in phrases like 嘘寒问暖 [xū hán wèn nuǎn] asking people if they feel hot (in summer) or cold (in winter) - inquiring after one's well-being, and 嘘叹 [xū tàn] sighing.
- 吹嘘 [chuī xū] to boast was a neutral phrase initially. It took on a negative connotation after the Northern and Southern Period.

沈 to sink [chén]

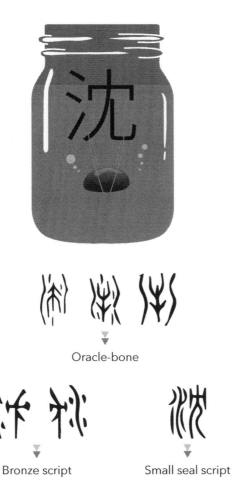

Oracle-bone

Bronze script

Small seal script

- This is a compound ideographic character. The oracle bone script consisted of two flowing lines symbolizing a river. In the middle was a cow with its head lowered. The black dots represented water.
- Its original meaning was *to let the cow sink into the river as a sacrificial offering to the River God.*
- The extended meaning refers to *an elevated place covered in water.*

初 original, the beginning of, first [chū]

Oracle-bone

Bronze script

Small seal script

- This is a compound ideographic character. The character's symbol on the left in its oracle bone script was a garment, and on the right was a knife. The idea was using a knife (the cutting tool) to make garments. Eventually, the character was extended to mean *the beginning of*.
- Later generations referred to *the garments of an official before he took office* as 初服 [chū fú]. His *court attire* was called 朝服 [cháo fú].
- People in ancient times divided the month into four parts. *The first to the seventh or eighth day* is called 初吉 [chū jí].

忧 to worry, to be anxious [yōu]

Oracle-bone   Bronze script   Small seal script

- The complex character is a compound ideograph denoting the idea of sorrow. Of the semantics in the oracle bone script, the symbol of a foot under the symbol of a person was very clear. The person's head was hung low, and his hand was poised to scratch his long hair.
- 丁忧 [dīng yōu] *the mourning period for deceased parents* was an important system for officials in ancient China. When the parent of an official passed away, the official was required to stop work and return to his hometown for a three-year mourning period.
- 忧 was regarded as the third most evil thing among the Six Evils in ancient times. As a result, the character's meaning was extended to denote *sickness* or *bereavement*.
- When the character is used to mean sickness, a more refined way of referring to an illness is 负薪之忧 [fù xīn zhī yōu] or 采薪之忧 [cǎi xīn zhī yōu], both meaning *sickness results in inability to work*.

言 word, speech [yán]

Oracle-bone   Bronze script   Small seal script

– 言 is a compound ideographic character. "言 is *speech or words spoken directly. When a discussion or debate is involved*, it is 语 [yǔ]."
– There are several different explanations for the oracle bone version of this character, none of which have been confirmed.

良 good [liáng]

Oracle-bone   Bronze script   Small seal script

– This is a pictographic character. Its oracle bone script was the image of a palace with exits leading to corridors on both sides.
– In ancient times, a woman who made her husband proud was referred to as 良. Subsequently, the character was extended to mean 良善 [liáng shàn] *kind*.

宋 a surname [sòng]

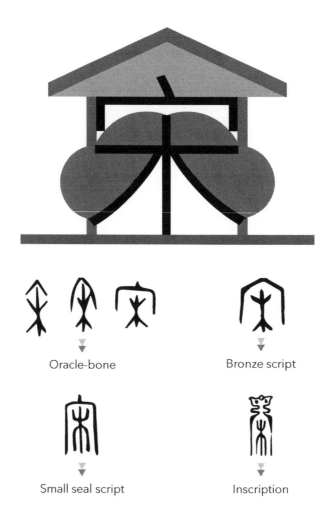

Oracle-bone

Bronze script

Small seal script

Inscription

- This is a compound ideographic character. The character's symbol in the oracle bone script was a roof. Below it was the image of a block of wood. The wood was placed in the house to refer to the people living there.
- The surname 宋 is one of the bigger family names in China.
- 商丘 [Shāng Qiū] is a historical, culture-rich city in Henan Province, also known as 宋. The name originated from a ritual ceremony for the worship of the sky and the sun.

迟 late, delay [chí]

Oracle-bone   Bronze script   Small seal script

- The complex form of this character is a compound ideograph. It denoted the idea of a person walking with another person on his back, implying the difficulty and slow speed of the action.
- Ancient poetry frequently used the phrase 迟迟 to add emphasis to the character. Examples are 行道迟迟 [xíng dào chí chí] *the path is tough*, and 威仪迟迟 [wēi yí chí chí] *poised and leisurely in manner.*

 to paint, to draw [huà]

Oracle-bone

Bronze script

Small seal script

— This character is a compound ideograph. The character's symbol in the oracle bone script was a hand holding a brush. Below it was a flowery pattern. The idea behind it was a hand drawing a picture.

— People in ancient times stated that 画 to draw was to create a boundary (or a frame). Subsequently, it was extended to mean adding colors and pictures for decoration. It was extended even further to mean stop.

— In the ancient world, when life was simple and legal requirements were low, it was very easy to govern the country. One would only need to 画地为牢 [huà dì wéi láo] draw a circle on the ground to serve as a prison, and 削木为吏 [xiāo mù wéi lì] carve a piece of wood and say it is the prison guard to do the job well. Both proverbs are used figuratively to mean almost as easy as ABC.

采 to pick [cǎi]

| Oracle-bone | Bronze script | Small seal script |

- This is a compound ideographic character. The character's symbol in the oracle bone script was a hand facing downward. Under the hand was a tree (wood). The idea behind it was a hand picking the leaves on a tree.
- The original idea was to *gently pick leaves and fruit.*
- The extended meaning of 采 is color.
- *The land of the ancient feudal bureaucrats* was called 采地 [cài dì] or 采邑 [cài yì].

委 to gather, to accumulate [wěi]

Oracle-bone

Small seal script

- This is a compound ideographic character. The oracle bone script was the stalk of a cereal plant bending its head, indicating that it was ripe for harvest. A woman half-kneeling half-sitting beside it denoted that the harvested crop was ready to be moved away. The original idea of 委 was to pile up harvested grains
- 委随 [wěi suí] *obedient*, and further *to submit*.
- The proverb 虚与委蛇 [xū yǔ wēi yí] means *pretend politeness and compliance*. The two characters in 委蛇 can be written as 逶迤 [wēi yí].

季 season, the end of an epoch [jì]

Oracle-bone

Bronze script

Small seal script

- This is a compound ideographic character. The oracle bone script was the stalk of a cereal plant, and below it was the symbol of a child. The main idea of the character was the young of the cereal plant. A saying in ancient times held that "a seedling denotes life. A grown cereal plant denotes elegance."
- 季 is extended to mean *the youngest in age* or *the last in line*.
- The last month of every season is also a 季. The term for *four seasons* is 四季 [sì jì].

周 circumference [zhōu]

Oracle-bone

Bronze script

Small seal script

- This is a pictographic character. The oracle bone script looked like a field of crops. The four black dots represented the crops.
- The Zhou tribe lived in the southwestern part of Jinshan. During the era of the ancient Gong Tan Fu, they moved to Zhou Yuan, to the foot of the present-day Qishan in Shaanxi. The name of the area was also the name of the people. They became the State of Zhou. The 周 of Zhou Yuan came from the shape of the farmland.
- The extended meanings are 稠密 [chóu mì] *dense*, and 周密 [zhōu mì] *thorough*.

服 to serve, to submit [fú]

Oracle-bone

Bronze script

Small seal script

- This is a compound ideographic character. The character's symbol in oracle bone script was a person in a half-kneeling position. To his right was a hand. To his left was a human sacrifice. The idea of the character was to surrender or to be engaged in a ceremonial ritual pertaining to worship.
- The Shang Dynasty had a system of internal and external services. The external service was for places outside of the capital city. The internal service was for the capital city and its suburbs, and was administered by the emperor himself.

宗 clan, ancestor [zōng]

Oracle-bone

Bronze script

Small seal script

- This is a compound ideographic character. The character's symbol in oracle bone script was a roof. Below it were two figures that looked like rocks or wooden rods put together to make an altar. The idea behind 宗 is an ancestral shrine.
- 祖 [zǔ] refers to *forefather*. Both the terms 始祖 [shǐ zǔ] *earliest forefathers* and 先祖 [xiān zǔ] *deceased grandfather, ancestry* are 宗.
- In the ancient genealogy system, 大宗 [dà zōng] refers to *the heir – the first son from the first wife and first son of his son.* The other sons and grandsons belonged to the 小宗 [xiǎo zōng] *the minor group in genealogy.*

享 to enjoy [xiǎng]

Oracle-bone   Bronze script   Small seal script

- This is a pictographic character. The character's symbol in oracle bone script was a cave for dwelling. In the middle were steps for the entrance and exit. Above was a roof as a shelter from rain.
- Emperor Zhou's ancestral worship ritual consisted of 六享 [liù xiǎng] *six sacrificial offerings*.

単 great [dān]

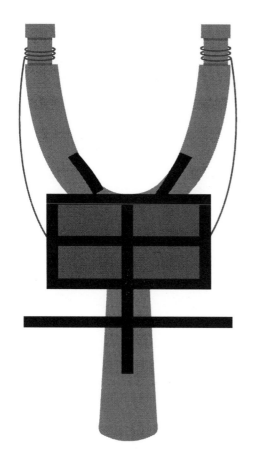

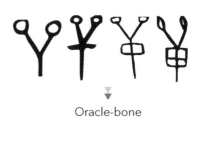

Oracle-bone

Bronze script

Small seal script

- This is a pictographic character. The character's symbol in oracle bone script was a double-prong wooden stick. A stone was tied to each prong to indicate that it was a tool for hunting. 单 means *big* or *great*.
- People in ancient times sat on mats on the floor. A rich man had more mats, and thick mats indicated important seats. Spirit worship only required one 'thick' or important seat.
- The character used in 名单 [míng dān] *name list*, 账单 [zhàng dān] *bill*, and 菜单 [cài dān] *menu* resulted from the idea of adding one important layer to another.

case, a small decorative box, armour [hán]

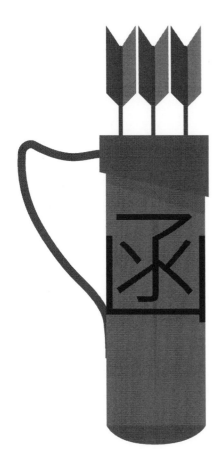

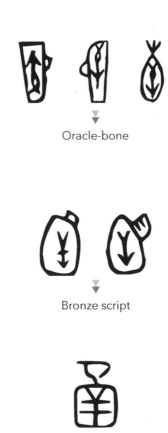

Oracle-bone

Bronze script

Small seal script

- This is a pictographic character. The character's symbol in oracle bone script was an arrow. The external part was a quiver. On the right of the quiver was a button used as a loop for hanging it on a wall.
- Armour in ancient times was initially made from leather. Subsequently, 圅 was used to mean *armour* and 圅人 [hán rén] referred to *a person who made armour*.
- 圅 extended its meaning from a container for arrows to *a small decorative box*, and from arrows being in the quiver to mean *include and contain (or accommodate)*.

艰 difficult, hard [jiān]

Oracle-bone

Bronze script

Small seal script

- The complex form of this character is a compound ideograph. The character's symbol in oracle bone script was a person in a kneeling position. On his left was a drum. His arms were out of sight under his body. The image indicated the cruel practice of burning human sacrifice as part of worship.
- The implication of the character was extended to mean *difficulty*, and later to mean *sinister*.

孟 eldest brother, the first month [mèng]

Bronze script   Small seal script

- This is a compound ideographic character. The character's symbol in oracle bone script was a basin (tub) for washing. In it was a newborn baby. "孟 refers to the eldest. The compounds in the character were 子 [zǐ] *son* and 皿 [mǐn] *vessel*. The former is used for semantic value and the latter is used for phonetic value."
- People in ancient times arranged siblings in this order: 孟, *first-born*, 仲 [zhòng] *second-born* and 季 [jì] *youngest*. Another regulation of this order was that the eldest son of the first wife received the title 伯 [bó] *the eldest of the brothers*. The title for the eldest son of the concubine was 孟.
- As the meaning of 孟 was extended from *the first in order* to *the beginning*, the first month of every season is also called 孟.

封 envelope, to close, to seal [fēng]

Oracle-bone   Bronze script   Small seal script

- This is a pictographic character. The character's symbol at the bottom of the oracle bone script was a mound of soil. Above it was a tree. The character referred to the land of the dukes and princes.
- 封 meant *to plant trees as a boundary to close up an area*. 建 [jiàn] was *to build a country*. Therefore 封建 [fēng jiàn] meant *to close the land to build the country*.
- Any mound of soil can be considered as 封, as in 封禅 [fēng shàn] *the grand ceremony for worshipping heaven on the mountain*.

省 to examine critically [xǐng] / to deduct, to economize [shěng]

Oracle-bone   Bronze script   Small seal script

- 省 [xǐng] is a compound ideograph. The oracle bone script was a large eye below a sprig of a grass, indicating the inspection of a tiny object or point.
- Oracle bone divination had repeated records of the observation of fields. The idea of external observation could be extended to *internal reflection* 反省 [fǎn xǐng]. 省 [shěng] was extended to mean *to remove, to reduce,* and *to omit.* 省视 [xǐng shì] was another extension of the character to denote *visiting and giving one's respect to the elders.*
- 省 [shěng] is used to refer to *a province.* In the Song Dynasty, the central government would send provincial government to 行省 [xíng shěng] *the name given to the area's highest administrative regions.* The short form of the phrase is just 省.

香 fragrant, sweet-smelling, savory [xiāng]

Oracle-bone

Small seal script

- This is a compound ideographic character. The character's symbol in oracle bone script was a bending sprig of wheat. Below it was a vessel for containing grain. Fragrance referred to the grains, and sweet-smelling referred to the grass.
- 馨香 [xīn xiāng] *smell of burning incense* is the phrase used for grain offerings to the deities.
- The original idea of 香 can be extended to refer to the sweet smells of plants, such as 沉香 [chén xiāng] *agarwood*, 檀香 [tán xiāng] *sandalwood*, and 丁香 [dīng xiāng] *clove*. It can also refer to the odor of animals, for example 麝香 [shè xiāng] *musk*.

侵 to invade, to intrude [qīn]

Oracle-bone

Bronze script

Small seal script

- This is a compound ideographic character. The character's symbol on the right of the oracle bone script was a hand holding a broom. On the left was the symbol of a cow with three dots above it. The original idea was *to advance gradually*. Its extended meaning was *invasion*.
- When warring troops were accompanied by drums, such attacks were called 伐 [fá] *to attack, to strike*. When there were no drums, they were called 侵 [qīn] *to intrude*. When the noise was light, it was called 袭 [xí] *to make a surprise attack*.
- In ancient times, *famine* was known as 大侵 [dà qīn]

宣 to declare, to proclaim [xuān]

Oracle-bone   Bronze script   Small seal script

- 宣 is a compound ideographic character. The character's symbol of the oracle bone character was a roof. The image of the coil under it denoted the decorative patterns found in palaces. The character referred to *the hall where the emperor issued decrees*.
- In ancient times, only the emperor's residential area was big and spacious, so it was called a 宣室 [xuān shì] *the hall where the emperor issues decrees*. The bright, high-ceilinged court was called 明堂 [míng táng] *the court where the emperor declares punishments, rewards, or instructions*.
- 宣榭 [xuān xiè] referred to *pavilions or terraces that were built in an elevated place* – the locations for events and activities related to martial arts. Subsequently, 宣 was used in 宣扬威武 [xuān yáng wēi wǔ] *mighty, powerful*.

室 a large room [shì]

Oracle-bone   Bronze script   Small seal script

- This is a compound ideographic character. The character's symbol in oracle bone script was a roof. In the middle was an arrow pointing downwards. The line at the bottom of the character represented the ground, carrying the idea of the arrow falling down towards it.
- Houses in ancient times were divided into three sections – the hall, the main house, and the side houses. The hall for receiving guests was the closest to the entrance, followed by the main house. Adjoining the main house were the side houses.
- The first wife lived in the main house as she was the 正室 [zhèng shì] *legal wife* (literally *main house*). The concubine lived in the side house. The title 偏房 [piān fáng] *concubine* (literally *side wing*) referred to her.

宫 palace [gōng]

Oracle-bone   Bronze script   Small seal script

- In prehistoric times, people lived in caves in the wilderness. Later generations began to build houses for shelter. After the Han Dynasty, only the emperor's abode could be called 宫 *a palace*.
- 宫 is a pictographic character. The character's symbol in oracle bone script was the outline of a house. Below were two squares that looked like ventilation windows on the slant of a roof. The actual meaning of 宫 was *a large room*.
- The character was also used to mean *circle around*, and was extended to mean *central*.
- The character was also used in the phrase 宫刑 [gōng xíng] *the punishment of castration*, one of the five punishments in ancient times. It was also used to refer to the cruel punishment of removing a woman's sexuality.

帝 emperor, the Supreme Being [dì]

Oracle-bone   Bronze script   Small seal script

- This is a pictographic character. The oracle bone version is a figure made up of three wooden sticks. The horizontal line with two short vertical lines indicated that the sticks were tied together. The vertical line at the top represented the heavens. The 禘祭 [dì jì] *a ritual ceremony for sacrificial offerings to the sky (heavens)* was performed outside the city.
- The Yin people originally carried out 禘祭 to worship the heavens, nature, and the four (all) directions. Later worship included deceased emperors.

突 sudden, to protrude [tū]

Oracle-bone

Ancient royal
seal script

Small seal script

– This is a compound ideograph. In oracle bone script, the dog was below. Above it was a cave-like image. Some scholars believe that the dog was a sacrificial offering and the cave-like image was a stove.
– People in ancient times referred to the chimney for smoke from the altar as 突 or 灶突 [zào tū] *stove chimney*.

逆 contrary, inverse [nì]

Oracle-bone

Bronze script

Small seal script

- This is a pictographic character. The character's symbol in oracle bone script was a person in an upside-down position. The idea behind it was *to meet with the intention of welcoming*.
- 逆旅 [nì lǚ] is an alternative name for *guest houses, hotels*.
- From 屰 [nì] *disobedient*, the character in phrases like 叛逆 [pàn nì] *rebel*, 讨逆 [tǎo nì] *to supress the rebels*, and 大逆不道 [dà nì bú dào] *to commit high treason*, took on a negative connotation.

秦 A state in the Zhou Dynasty, the Qin Dynasty [qín]

Oracle-bone   Bronze script   Small seal script

- This is a compound ideographic character. The character's symbol in oracle bone script was a pair of hands holding a pestle. Below it were sprigs of cereal plants bending their heads, indicating they were ripe and ready. The idea behind the character was the husking of the grains.
- In ancient India, China was known as Zhī Nà, which sounded like 秦.

晋 to advance, to promote, to enter [jìn]

| Oracle-bone | Bronze script | Small seal script |

— This is a compound ideographic character. The character's symbol in oracle bone script consisted of arrows with arrowheads. Below was a container, to denote the idea of inserting the arrows into a receptacle.

— The character's meaning can be extended to denote *to exit*, *to rise*, or *to promote*. Both the phrases 晋升 [jìn shēng] and 晋级 [jìn jí] mean *to promote to a higher office*.

— After the State of Jin relocated to the River Jin, it took the name 晋.

索 a large rope [suǒ]

Oracle-bone   Bronze script   Small seal script

- This is a pictographic character. The character's symbol in oracle bone script was an image of two straw strings twisted together into one rope.
- Stems of grass can be made into a rope. Thicker ropes are called 索, while thinner ones are known as 绳 [shéng] *strings*.
- During a famine in the Zhou Dynasty, the people asked for blessings from the spirit world. This was called 索鬼神 [suǒ guǐ shén] *calling on supernatural beings*.
- 索 can be extended to refer to *separation*. The idea of a rope can also be extended to cover *braids*.

夏 summer [xià]

Bronze script   Small seal script

- This is a pictograph. Its oracle bone script has not been interpreted.
- Legends lauded Dayu as a man with a great talent for writing music. His compositions were often entitled 'Summer'.
- The elaborate farming celebrations of summer extended the meaning of the character to denote *grand, magnificent*. Kong Anguo explained, "The elegant attire of officials depicts grandeur (华); a country that is big depicts prosperity (夏)." That was how ancient China came to be known as 华夏 [huá xià].

殷 flourishing, abundant [yīn]

Oracle-bone

Bronze script

Small seal script

- The original idea of this character was delivering a child either through Caesarean section or by natural birth. It was later extended to mean *new birth*.
- 殷商 [yīn shāng], the name of the Shang Dynasty, denoted a new empire, a new birth, and an imperial revival.
- The meaning of the character 殷 was extended to denote *grand, abundant*.
- The surname 殷 originated in the Shang Dynasty.

唐 to exaggerate [táng]

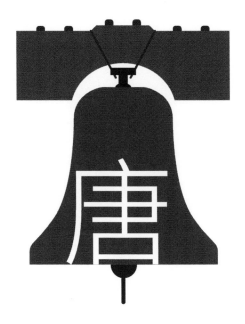

Oracle-bone

Bronze script

Small seal script

- This is a pictographic character. The shape of the oracle bone script was a bell with a clapper at the bottom. The idea of the character was *extension, vast and mighty*.
- The phrase 荒唐 [huāng táng] *absurd, grossly exaggerated* has the idea of *extension, to be without boundary*.
- The Tang Dynasty was named after its founding monarch, Emperor Tang Gaozu (Li Yuan), who inherited the title Duke of Tang from his grandfather.

曹 people of the same kind, ministry officials [cáo]

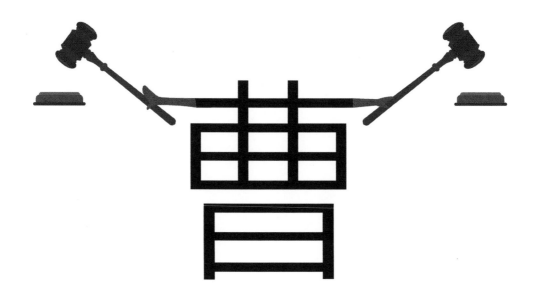

Oracle-bone   Bronze script   Small seal script

- This is a compound ideograph. The character's symbols in oracle bone script were two iterations of the character 东 [dōng] *east*. Below was the symbol of a mouth.
- The two pockets on the character 曹 stood for criminal litigation charges and civil law litigation charges respectively. Both were handed to the government. Both parties presented their cases and the judge pronounced judgement, implied by the 'mouth' in the character. It later developed to 曰 [yuē] to represent the judgement. "Jail is represented by the two parties (referring to 曹) - the accuser and the defendant." That was how the character acquired its meaning.
- The implication of the judicial system in the character 曹 extended its meaning to *judiciary authorities*, as in 法曹 [fǎ cáo] *judges*.

嗇 harvest, stingy [sè]

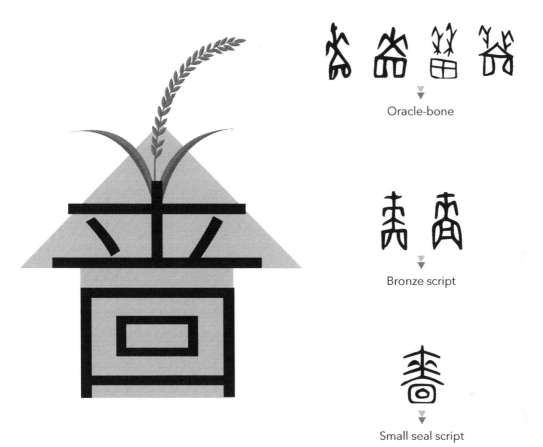

Oracle-bone

Bronze script

Small seal script

— The complex form of this character is a compound ideograph. The character's symbol in oracle bone script was a sprig of cereal above a granary. The idea behind it was storing grains and harvested crops in storehouses. The primary meaning is *harvesting crops*.

— An extension of the character is 爱嗇 [ài sè], which has the same meaning as 爱惜 [ài xī] *to cherish*.

— 吝嗇 [lìn sè] was one of the virtues of Mother Earth. However, the phrase gradually lost its original meaning. When it was used for people, it took on a negative connotation.

春 to pound, pestle [chōng]

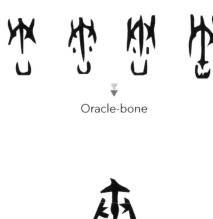

Oracle-bone

Bronze script

Small seal script

- This is a compound ideographic character. Above the symbol for a stone mortar in the oracle bone script were two hands holding on to a pestle. The idea behind it was hands pounding or grinding grains. The original meaning was *to pound millet*.
- According to records in *Zhou Li (The Rites of Zhou)*, there was a job for a person working with a pestle in the Zhou Dynasty.
- Another explanation of the character is *to collide*.

蛊 poison, venom, to bewitch [gǔ]

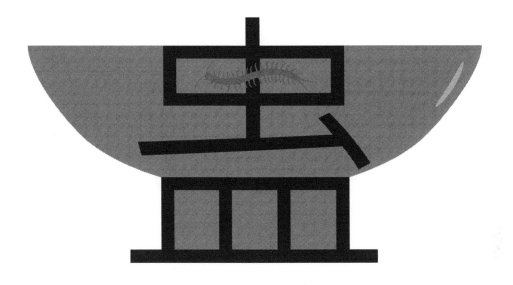

Oracle-bone

Houma Covenant
(Spring and Autumn Period)
侯马盟书 (c. 1400 BC)

Small seal script

- This is a compound ideographic character. The character's symbol in oracle bone script was a vessel containing two worms. The original definition was *roundworm infection*.
- The character was extended to mean *to confuse, to harm*.

豚 pig [tún]

| Oracle-bone | Bronze script | Small seal script |

- This is a compound ideograph. The oracle bone script was a symbol of a pig with its belly facing left. On the left was a piece of pork belly, implying an offering as part of worship rites.
- During the Zhou Dynasty, there was a position for an official who oversaw catering (a chef). "Spring is the time to eat young pigs. When used for cooking, the fats (oils) from the young pig make the food very appetizing (aromatic)."
- There were specific names given to animal sacrifices used in ancestral worship. 刚鬣 [gāng liè] were *pigs that were not castrated*, while 腯肥 [tú féi] referred to *pigs that were castrated*.

商 trade, business [shāng]

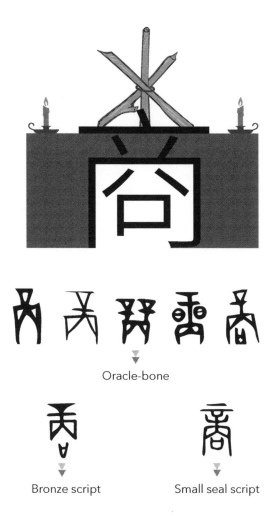

Oracle-bone

Bronze script

Small seal script

- This is a compound ideographic character. The character's symbol in oracle bone script was a stand or an altar. On it was a bundle of wooden sticks, below a horizontal line representing the sky. The idea behind the character was the burning of sticks on an altar to worship the heavens and the stars.
- In ancient ancestral temple worship, the ritual of offering dried fish was known as 商祭 [shāng jì] *worship rites of the Shang Period.*

宿 to stay overnight, to lodge for the night [sù]

Oracle-bone

Bronze script

Small seal script

- This is a pictographic character. The character's symbol in oracle bone script was a person on a straw mat, indicating sleeping for the night.
- The term 星宿 [xīng xiù] *constellation* came from the ancient saying, "Even the stars stop and stay at their resting place".

旋 to revolve, to return [xuán]

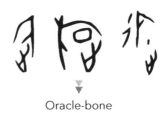

Oracle-bone

Bronze script

Small seal script

– This is a compound ideographic character. The character's symbol in oracle bone script was a flag. On the flag pole were two waving streamers. Below was a foot. The focus of the character was the foot (feet) moving with the flag, denoting the idea of *shifting*.

– 旋 was the gesture of a greeting salute in ancient times.

– From the idea of shifting, the character was extended to mean *return*, as in *return in victory*.

朝 dynasty, morning [cháo]

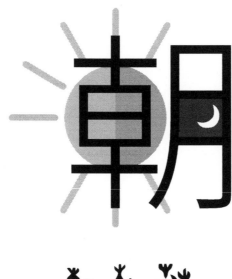

Oracle-bone

Bronze script

Small seal script

- This is a compound ideographic character. The character's symbol on the top and bottom left of the oracle bone script was grass. In the middle was the sun, and on the right was the moon. The character referred to the time when the sun had just risen but the moon had not totally disappeared. The idea behind it was *dawn, the break of day.*
- During the Xia, Shang, and Zhou Dynasties, the heaven-worshipping ritual was performed on the vernal equinox. The term for this ceremony was 郊祭 [jiāo jì] or 朝日 [zhāo rì].
- The phrase 朝觐 [cháo jìn] was used for *the meetings of the officials with the emperor in feudal times (an audience with the emperor). Meetings in spring* were called 朝, and *meetings in autumn* were called 觐 [jìn].

鲁 foolish, vulgar [lǔ]

Oracle-bone   Bronze script   Small seal script

- This is a compound ideographic character. The character's symbol in oracle bone script was a fish. Below it was a cooking pot. The idea behind it was that the fish was tasty. From the original idea, it was extended to mean *a word of praise*.
- The people of the State of Lu were *simple and dull*. The term 鲁 was subsequently extended to mean *stupid, rough*. 鲁莽 [lǔ mǎng] *reckless* is a further extension of the character.

媚 to fawn over, to flatter, to charm [mèi]

Oracle-bone

Bronze script

Small seal script

– This is a pictographic ideograph. The character's symbol in oracle bone script was a woman kneeling. Above her was an emphasized version of her eye, with distinctive lashes. The idea behind it was that girls with big eyes and beautiful brows were more popular.

– In later generations, phrases containing this character took on negative connotations.

粪 excrement, dung [fèn]

Oracle-bone

Warring States
seal script 战国印文

Small seal script

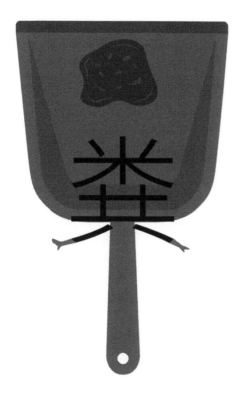

- This is a compound ideographic character. The character's symbol at the bottom of the oracle bone script was a pair of hands below a dustpan. The idea behind it was hands using a dustpan to clear filth, meaning *to clean up*.
- *Zhou Li – Cao Ren (The Rites of Zhou)* categorized soil into nine types. Grains for planting were pre-mixed with juice from boiling nine types of animal bones, and were then sowed in specific types of soil. This farming practice was known as 粪种 [fèn zhǒng].

裘 fur coat [qiú]

Oracle-bone   Bronze script   Small seal script

– This is a pictographic character. The character's symbol at the top of the oracle bone script was a shirt collar. Below was a fur garment.

– In ancient times, there were etiquette regulations pertaining to social status and fur garments. The common people were not allowed to wear fur coats of higher grades. They could only wear coats made from sheep and dogs. They were not required to remove their outer coats to reveal the non-accessorized garments underneath.

遣 to send off, to dispatch [qiǎn]

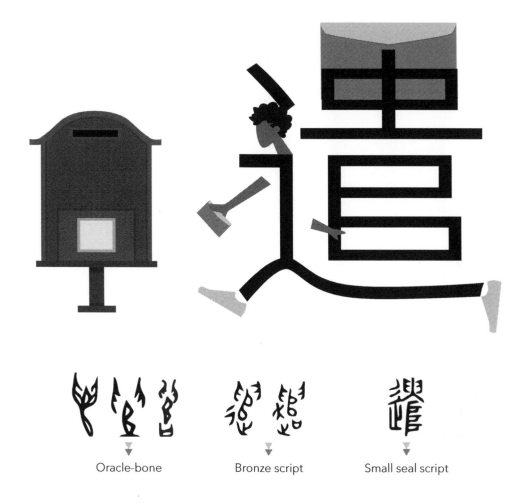

| Oracle-bone | Bronze script | Small seal script |

- This is a compound ideographic character. The character's symbol on the top of the oracle bone script was a pair of hands holding a piece of meat that was to be used as an offering in worship. The character denoted the idea of using animals as a sacrifice.
- From the idea of 遣奠 [qiǎn diàn] *a dead body about to be buried,* the character 遣 was extended to mean *to send off, to exile.*

雍 harmony [yōng]

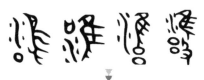

Oracle-bone

Bronze script

Small seal script

- This character was originally a compound ideograph - 雝. The character's symbol on the top of the oracle bone script was a bird, denoting a wagtail looking for food by the marshes.
- During the Eastern Zhou Dynasty, the emperor set up an institution called the 辟雍 [pì yōng] *Imperial University*.
- From the idea of the wagtail's humming, the character 雍 extended its meaning to *musical movement (part of a music composition)*.

豢 to feed, to groom [huàn]

Oracle-bone   Small seal script

- This is a compound ideographic character. The character's symbol in oracle bone script was a pig lying down. On both sides were two hands, denoting the idea of caring for the pig. The character meant *rearing a pig with grain in a sty.*
- The pig was one of the six earliest domesticated animals in ancient China. Therefore, the character was generalized to mean *raising livestock.*

辟 to break, incisive [pì]

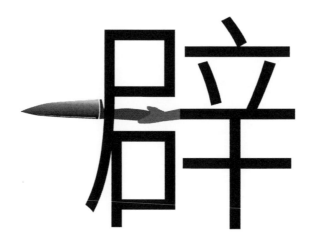

Oracle-bone

Bronze script

Small seal script

– This is a compound ideographic character. The character's symbol in oracle bone script was a person kneeling. On the other side was a knife used in executions. The idea behind it was *to carry out the death penalty*. The meaning of the character was extended to refer to criminal charges such as 大辟 [**dà pì**] *capital punishment like decapitation*.
– 辟 was later used in the titles of monarchs.

嘉 fine, good, praise [jiā]

Bronze script

Small seal script

— This is a compound ideographic character, referring to the beauty of eating and drinking.

— During the Zhou Dynasty, etiquette and ceremonial rites were divided into five types, one of which was 嘉礼 [jiā lǐ] *a banquet for celebration.* This was set up with the intention of inspiring kindness and good-feeling.

— There was a form of discipline in the Zhou Dynasty called the *Jiashi Punishment,* which involved making a criminal sit on a rock, both as a method of public warning, and to force him to reflect on his actions.

輿 carriage, sedan chair [yú]

Oracle-bone

Stone script of Qin
(The Curse of Chu)
秦代石刻《诅楚文》

Small seal script

- This is a pictographic character. The character's symbol in oracle bone script consisted of four hands. In the middle was a carriage and a log. The idea behind the character was a carriage that needed to be pushed or pulled by people.
- The character was used to mean *delivery or* to carry. Ancient China referred to *territory maps* as 舆图 [yú tú] or 舆地图 [yú dì tú].
- 乘舆 [chéng yú] used to denote *the sedan chair that the emperor, the dukes, and the princes rode on*. Later it was used to refer to *the emperor*.

膏 fat, ointment, cream [gāo]

Oracle-bone

Ancient pottery inscriptions
(Pre-Qin Period) 古陶文

Small seal script

- This is a compound ideograph. The character's symbol at the bottom of the oracle bone script was meat. Above it was the image of a high roof, representing a temple for ancestral worship used by the emperor, princes, and dukes. The idea behind it was *the oil used in worship rituals*.
- The meaning of the character was extended to refer to meat fat. It was further extended to mean *fertile*.

霍 quickly, suddenly [huò]

Oracle-bone

Bronze script

Small seal script

- This is a compound ideographic character. The character's symbol in oracle bone script was rain. Below it was the image of three birds. The idea behind it was birds fluttering in the rain.
- The original meaning of 挥霍 [huī huò] was *rapid, swift*. It was later used negatively to mean *to squander*.

盥 washing (especially hands) [guàn]

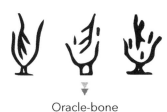

Oracle-bone

Bronze script

Small seal script

— This is a compound ideographic character. The character's symbol in oracle bone script was a wash basin with a hand in it, denoting the washing of hands in a basin. Although it referred explicitly to the washing of hands, the idea behind it was that another person was pouring water over the subject's hands, meaning that handwashing was done by a third party.

— People in ancient time categorized washing into different types. 进盥 [jìn guàn] *the washing of hands for parents* was a daily morning activity.

襄 to assist, to help [xiāng]

Oracle-bone

Ancient text

Three Body Stone Classic
(Warring States)
三体石经 (C. AD 220)

Small seal script

- This is a compound ideographic character. The oracle bone script was a symbol meaning *to remove clothes before ploughing the land*.
- The meaning of the character was extended to denote *to assist*. It also meant *complete, achievement*. It was extended again to mean *to repeat*.

鑊 wok, kettle [huò]

Oracle-bone

Bronze script

Small seal script

— This is a compound ideographic character. The outer shape of the oracle bone script was the symbol of a tripod-shaped utensil. In it was the image of a bird. The idea behind it was the cooking of a bird.
— People in ancient times used a 鼎鑊 [dǐng huò] *cauldron* to make tea.

BIO OF XU HUI

Born in 1969, Xu Hui is a freelance writer, presently residing in Dali, Yunnan. He was the chief editor for *Temperament of the Sixties*, *The Backdoor of Chinese History*, and other works, and co-author of *The New Shuowen Interpretation*, *The Chinese Language Dictionary*, and the series *Looking at History the Fun Way*. His books include *The Art of Body Charm: Body Politics in Chinese History*, *Troubled Times Specimens: Personality Disorder in Chinese History*, *The Whip of Troubled Times: Thirty Most Controversial People in Chinese History*, *The Most Misunderstood Idioms of the Chinese People*, and *Enlightening Interpretation of Chinese Phrases*.

BIO OF JULIE LOO

Julie Loo, a former principal of Shanghai Singapore International School, XuHui Campus, has been in the education field in Singapore and Shanghai for more than 28 years. Being an educator, she shares the author's passion in wanting people learning Chinese Language to appreciate the beauty of the language.